AMERICAN MASSIF

NICHOLAS REGIACORTE

American Massif follows the first stages of one American Mastodon in his attempts to evolve. His life begins to resemble a human life. His mother appears human. His wife and children, human. His own birthplace and childhood. His appetites, sins, faith, cynicism, big plans. All apparently human.

The massif's landscapes are as varied as pinewoods, clay hills and prairie, but grow more abstract. In his naive way, A.M. moves through or ponders the Higgs Field, art, national and family states of emergency. From his own house to an airport, from volcano to museum, he goes foraging for images good enough to eat, for friends, for antidotes to apocalypse.

Perhaps no more human by the end, A.M. is re-released into the world like a new habitat—however threatened. Rather, like the Pompeian who returns to her city, the Mastodon comes into his own.

"Brimming with insights and whimsy while often leaving us on the edge so subtly we don't know how we got there, Nick Regiacorte's *American Massif* is a book that simply cannot be pigeon-holed. This is work from a patient writer who has taken his time to bring us this collection of well- wrought, passionate observations of the natural world which includes human making and thought. We begin our reading with an unspoken nod to the President whose stone face resides on that most American of edifices, Mount Rushmore. Jefferson's obsession with claiming the living 'American Mastadon' is never directly addressed, but reappears in this collection as if a plea or warning. Just as the ephemeral grasses sway in the wind, the mastodon sways on its forelegs toward extinction and revival through the unearthing of its bones, both actions leading to profound exercises of the imagination. *American Massif* does not mean to be read as science, as facts. Instead here is a highly lyrical, unpredictable collection of poetry that takes surprising leaps of thought, swerving across a broad swath of landscapes, eras, philosophies, and topics, moving deftly from St. Sebastian to Van Gogh, Dayton, Ohio to Mr. Cogito, art to the garden. In some sense it reads as a natural history that covers species and soil, but it expands into an *ars urbana* in its cosmopolitan insights, covering just enough to make the reading rich and engaging. In 'Pompeiian,' Regiacorte notes, 'the secret is always that you are not/perishable.' Which is one of the central concerns of this collection, What remains *and* what does that mean? This is a daring book of Whitmanesque measure, that explores personal and collective histories from vantages as varied as the mastodon and the father whose child is growing up faster than he can track. It will keep you rereading and discovering more each time. Regiacorte is that rarest of writers whose work refuses to privilege the separation of 'I' from 'you'; this I is 'we,' all of us, every living creature, in all of our fears and curiosity, violence and vulnerability."

—Vievee Francis, author of *Forest Primeval*

"As John Ashbery once avowed, and prophetically, 'we are fabulous beasts after all.' In *American Massif*, Nicholas Regiacorte takes the full measure of that prophecy by setting it into vivid motion across the American earth. Along the way, we are dearly reminded that the ordinary light of our common day is ravishing, that the familiar nets of our common language sparkle, as after a morning rain. While there is pain here, and outrage, a fabulous delight persists. This is a heartening, brilliant collection."

—Donald Revell, author of *White Campion*

"Nicholas Regiacorte's *American Massif* is a stunning book with an extraordinary reach. Bearing lyrical witness to the grit particulars of embodiment and extinction, Regiacorte examines with a keen intimacy both the wild and the domestic, weaving a thread from the present moment back to bygone epochs. With a vivid style, *American Massif* features a highly original, urgent kind of concentration: 'In the heart of my woods / I will open / for you alone a bright circle of / grasses whose / entrance will be guarded by a / seeping maple / and marked by the unearthed cheekbone of /a boulder...' In these highly pressurized poems, Regiacorte manages to halt traffic at the intersection of time and nature, personal and animal, emergence and extinction. This is a fantastic book of poetry!"

—Christopher Salerno, author of *The Man Grave*

"At first it may seem too 'on the nose' to speak of our perilous shifting climate through the voice of a mastodon, 'the elephant in the room' as it were. But Regiacorte's exquisite, lush lines swept my doubt away. For there is abundant humanity at the heart of this book. 'In the heart of my woods I will open for you alone a bright circle of grasses...' In all the ways that poetry can sway us with its art, this collection does deeply move me. 'Spearing to the core.' Thankfully an elephant never forgets."

—D.A. Powell, author of *Repast*

AMERICAN MASSIF

NICHOLAS REGIACORTE

TUPELO PRESS

NORTH ADAMS, MASSACHUSETTS

American Massif
Copyright © 2022 Nicholas Regiacorte. All rights reserved.
ISBN: 978-1-946482-70-9

Library of Congress Cataloging-in-Publication Data
Names: Regiacorte, Nicholas, 1974- author.
Title: American massif / Nicholas Regiacorte.
Description: First paperback edition. | North Adams, Massachusetts :
Tupelo Press, [2022]
Identifiers: LCCN 2021062378 | ISBN 9781946482709 (trade paperback)
Subjects: LCSH: Mastodons--Poetry.
Classification: LCC PS3618.E4485 A84 2022 | DDC 811/.6--dc23/eng/20220202
LC record available at https://lccn.loc.gov/2021062378

Cover image:
"Siamesis Unfurling Sails," photograph (medium: gelatin silver print) by
Lena Herzog of "Siamesis 2010," by Theo Jansen, (medium: PVC, tie wrap,
plastic, dracon), Netherlands, period "Suicideem 2009-2011."
Copyright © 2010 Lena Herzog. Used by permission.

Cover and text design by Allison O'Keefe

First paperback edition May 2022.

Tupelo Press
P.O. Box 1767
North Adams, Massachusetts 01247
(413) 664-9611 / Fax: (413) 664-9711
editor@tupelopress.org / www.tupelopress.org

Tupelo Press is an award-winning independent literary press that publishes
fine fiction, non-fiction, and poetry in books that are a joy to hold as well as
read. Tupelo Press is a registered 501(c)(3) nonprofit organization, and we rely
on public support to carry out our mission of publishing extraordinary work
that may be outside the realm of the large commercial publishers. Financial
donations are welcome and are tax deductible.

CONTENTS

Every thought raises flame

  for the one with a straw tail.

  —after the Vastese proverb

☦

American Mastodon

Nous somme tous sauvages.[i]

I always know weather
seven feet before I enter it
tusking into a day
like any other

but how can I convey
a sense of my girth and
melancholy yes
fattening on
the same grind
of corn

I'm no mammoth but
look at these molars
I could grind an entire
mill's worth of flour
why don't you

bake me my Nonna's bread
but you do you did
without even a brick oven
I remember

dear one it's not mood
it's congress it's
climate that catches
up with me

who couldn't outrun
a cloud well who could
I know I know.

I'm no terrorist I just have to
get down to
my mother who is sick but the agent
says Okay
we'll sort this out in the basement
Look I say
pulling bills from my change purse
like a magic
hanky look at this mouth sprung
wide open
this money but nothing vouches Amen amen
if you will only
come with us But you see she is the one
who crushed wasps
in her hand she always uses too
small a knife
for too large an onion she invented
Kettle Cove
Tut-tut if you'll calm down they say
two men to a tusk
Kettle Cove and that jetty the whole
idea of jetty
that splits the current and shelters
gentle beach
Suresure you're friendly aren't you
now three now
four men to a tusk wanding my
earflaps for IED's
She invented the *Pietà* with those flaking
palms
her nerves burning inside out her hands
flaking open
and bleeding How many of you are
in there
they say to my tail and probing I feel
the pressure
build on my spine like to birth
and steps
underfoot Ever heard of Pietà
Mercy
mercy yes we'll show you some
mercy sir
right away right this way.

I miss my little bipeds
for whom all the world's disparate falls
sprung from one great
fountain! What imaginations they had—
not only to ape but
in time to raise each thing above itself
why wouldn't I
lie down after all how earnestly
they pursued me
how unassuming their spears
but straight
ribwise & sharp how admirable
their cause
I imagine & industry in quartering me
employing every piece
tail to trunk eyes ears my ivories of
course into which
they might (one day) hollow out
architectures
carving little ivory baldachins
over miniature
ivory altars delicate cups
over invisible
ivory crypts why why wouldn't I
put death
behind me instead racing across
the river again
and again for cover watching the
tree-line for movement
my 40-pound heart raising the dust
beneath their feet.

domesticus

Head on I was an anvil
or enraptured
cross-eyed to see myself counting
rings down or
rings up
from the grasping & spouting o
every single
thing seemed cornered by
my falling or raised
proboscis eyeing
everything all tilt and if
I didn't watch it
skewered—
I lanced my letter my
sandwich
my poor dog Lupo
a lonely life
if not for you who found me
in profile a massif
and led me
out into this bog wading out
and driving
down through mud to be
like a forest of
larch trees new ground upon
which you'd raise
your palaces with canals in
between and bridges
over them an entire Sea
Republic though
subject as we knew to plagues
and I didn't want
any plagues on my back but
think of Santa Maria
della Salute
you said floating domes
in honor of
our survival IF we
survive I said
and that's a big IF
Okay then let's start with

a city lot a
modest two-bedroom
here and
good light from
the south.

I scaled the volcano but found myself
wading into lava-flow
at least in theory and cracking
jokes when I heard
Cocco through the fog Where are you
you crazy bastard
but I stayed quiet basked only then in the glow
and memory of slope-
flowers blue-green spurge and
Etna Broom yellow
that we'd snapped off for all our mothers before
the summit charred up
then clouded over could I actually live
on the thought of
bougainvillea or prickly pear while Cocco
and Claire kept calling
in a panic all cloud and the guide too
lost they must descend
shouting We must descend from the rim
and grandest discovery now
all to myself succored by how bright all
matter before it cools
before all pitch the hungry mastodon tossing
the understory for cones
and before that half-lost in woods little Nicky
cooling his feet among minnows.

in which the conceit of himself weighs on his prospects for happiness

Someone will
doubt my right to just be
so large

Is that all, Oh and
the whole trunk & tusk
thing?

Be the elephant in the room
if you want only don't be
that one

but it's no ruse
to be the only Pleistocene
in a loving but
Holocene house

where a suppressed laugh
sob growl makes
the whole frame shrink
in around

the unexploded shell
of me—

when chairs stutter back
from the table

dinner goes pale in each dish

floorboards
down the hall choke
on word of

my unsecret and self-
immolent
wish

—everyone's face
even the baby's
ruddied with love and
terror.

JDAM[ii]

Before a round vacuum
of light, at the wedding party in Qalai Niazi,
left forty pairs
of shoes on the crater rim, before impact, each
guest ascended into
a clean mind, we may imagine, algorithms of
thought & action fell out
clearly, the missile untangled all
bloodlines from fault.

You cannot start garlic in the pan, you can't
start nasturtiums in
the barrel, call your mother or friends
on Dayton for
the littlest thing, I can't so much as open
a page of Mr. Cogito, there's no
secret prayer, grudge, coveting, sarcastic song, talking
an old roommate
out of it, split second of despair for a
diagnosis, disgust
for a grand national deed, you can't

wake the floorboards
ahead of me, the south window & fresh shares of
crabapple, redstart
threading the lilac, sink and fogged mirror finally to
hold my face, and you
can't hold my face, no "Fall on us" or, to the hills
"Cover us," no walk

eastward, war prison turned hospital
turned sanitarium, or
southward the brickyard, Birthplace, zoo of radiators,
crack house
turned meth house, delicate
roofs of our restored Victorians, GABES PAWN,
Corpus, CONEY ISLAND
"moral lights" hushing out around us, no
giddy sighting
of you walking northward—a thing I've spoked

with scissor holiness, no
hidden smack of a kiss without their rising all
together into
the baroque and too-shallow cloud
of our first defense.

Grotto [Igneous]

Stromboli

The mountain revs to a point
like a jet that fails then
coughs up its slag in broad day a
dull climax of
snapping, fallout of sulfur, and
steam that uncoils
from a bomb that tumbles to seacalms
and cracks. Life here
keeps time with eruptions and,
behind our backs, wrath
dives quietly into the waters like
sludge, pushing
dark limits deeper. Once taut
fears grow slack
and we build new houses where
we find new hill.
Some nights I'll look up
for the spectacle
of embers—Ella might call me,
we stop eating
or drop whatever we are doing.
We'll look up from
a kiss, remember what the sound
means, turn back
wary and sleep. We loosen our
arms but mindfully
within the edges of bed. The
scored path slows—
in a cold afterlife beneath us,
where it is hid.

‡

Higgs Field Theories

I

dark boughs and our house soak in
all I know dark wings
slow to rise as the water goes
a long time filtered
through combs of thought warming
groundward as
our heads in the rain our roof
warms rains
unrousing the neighbors and me
if not for some
thunder to trouble bottles in a window
thinking

Aren't they ours? not our bottles?
not our slow rain?
Ella didn't toss just now, nor the baby?
He has tossed
off his covers. The storm has come to
visit, the wolf to
visit when the lamb shrugs. What right have I
to say it,
"the glass bottles' notes" or
"slow rain envelops"?
They're no one else's bottles clinking
in the stair well window
no more than anyone else's jagged toenail
that split her heel,
anyone else's wife bolting upright when
a clap hits the spruce,
just anyone's boy snorting in his sleep,
anyone else's
spruce, clap of thunder, look back from
the flash, a room of flash

sheets aflash to mean a bed standing
on flashing boards
a nightstand useless lamp

lampshade
and the Spanish landscape now a gouge
in white
the other windows gouged out
by the burst of light
where our birch must see could it see
the delicate shadow of
itself we see pressed like the shuddering world's
nerve into glass and curtain

Any physicist worth his particles
as any good Lupo
knows the field one must cross for
bone and blood
without naming or needing to name it
the field that
nauseates to break; for the infant
Campione
his mother makes a field

like the muddy infield of the Mabel I Wilson school
baseball diamond
across which this boy will run alone until
the universe, seizing
upon every curiosity, sucks the shoes
from his feet toc-tock
swallows the prints and feet ahead—for it
must have them.

To say I remember it, the herd
of boys stopping to
crowd the spectacle into being
to taunt me by
chanting; stranded in the
mud, their
standing in the grass, only one
of them will not
vanish—to say only one for certain, not naming
names—is where
I break one field to gain another.

3

Spearing to the core and living
off a day's pink slabs
now that's a childhood ever since
you brought up the end

of a line after friends
dragging your finger the length of the aisle
to receive the blessed
sacrament or in an arctic museum

single-file to leave your line
across blue light
behind which life-like bi-peds
squatted around a
lump of meat a fireless pit

a long line of yourself in time-
lapse now visits
all your life's mysteries
frozen in the
documentus momentus from
a cousin life
in the hospital garden with the
Argentine girl
to the dimly lit and actual room where
this one boy slipped

into the world whose sky's soft as the roof
of his own mouth
and close. What a marvel to you for whom
the day won't come down
easy, all mastodon. But for him

for the kid
how one word just one
flints up
from his lips and fells it
instantly
without piercing its hide.

4

I hate marshes, my mother says
           midway through
Scarborough's
                 green steeped in
greener where its rivers wind,
           Ella and the baby dozing
in back. Is it the slow water
                 and quiet, slow-
tick of mouths in the mud?
           obscene concavities of mud
eating away under
                a sure-footing
and wildflowers—which thrills me!
           tugging me
to the shoulder
                without slowing.
She admits *They are beautiful*
           but I hate 'em.

5

Call him Trade
or Towers
call him 34th
or Miner
name him Shorebird
for the Deepwater no
Pluto for Pluto all
but dissolved like a tablet
in space name him Tablet or
Streaming no
Glacial I say
or Drift now
Haiti now Mudslide
Oh please she says
Name him Jobs
Newtown now Chamber
name him Ferguson now
Emanuel now Pulse
Come on she says
but I say Acres now
Claimed now Homes
He's almost
three but Collider I say
Boson
or Field just as
she catches our boy
in the blue pullover—
where is your head? now
where are those
little hands?

Clawfoot

out back we collect snow in it
we keep ducklings
and I learn to swim in its
steadied waters
we clean tomatoes and trout Dad cleans a deer
right over it
dark blood draining into frozen grass
we try stomping

grapes in it long before the winepress
and before he is stolen
from our woods we wash Scanner in it
soak corroded hinges in
an agent in it until their cries quiet
we pretend to ride out
a Flood rehearsing all of our possessions
into it to begin with
our mother needs her Pietà
or her Singer

the pale blue lamb in the tubwhite together
their own proverb
and all the canning all sleeved installments of
gospel sarcophagus-piano
and I cry for the laundry chute where I'd hidden
between floors to
confound all seekers but we'll need the
wheelbarrow and
Dad's rifle my brother says

wants his old Yamaha 400 and
near-death
has to have Mazziotti's accordion
and the song that
got us here my sister must have the oregano
& low window
Little Sebago's shoreline
and lost camp
then again I was born here sickly so
we forgive one closet

its scrawlings and the stairwell
I survived
twice—I mustn't forget to plug
the drain now

catch every needle in the junk drawer
every flower from
the front bed bleeding hearts lily
of the valley and near
vineyard (not yet uprooted)
the peach tree
(before winter's mice)
the pear plum all
over-bearing and replant them
each in this tub

while we're at it the whole woods tugged
by its creek down to
low-tide and mud we'll want room
to slog out in and dig
for steamers we'll want a place to eat
again a table
butter and forks room for dessert—
wild blueberries
knowing the tub must founder
under us
and our huge bellies at any minute

jostling open new space the rumor
of space opening
new space for one's murdered Rita
for one's plotting Atta
one's drunk and threats from the den
one's adulteress
but now you my love and what will you want
if not the car
and your father before the wreck
if not Modesto's
yeasty leaves good oil a good starter for

sourdough at least good fish and a place
to dive kids together—
into the Saco or at the foot of Bear's Head
and terraced lemon groves
those fresh green waters and not wanting to
climb back into
Gaetano's boat without the waves as though
they were unwanted strays—
Can we keep them? you say arms wide
They seem to know us—Look—
eating from your hands
they roll over—and After all our children will
be born into this tub
and need bathing they will be born here
and need—friends.

Grotto Expanding at an Accelerating Rate

A cabinet that just fit us wants,
a closet wants, then this room
room enough to take one more and
wider table for the bottle, from
whose green mouth we're still expecting
the *Good Word*.

Paranoia and dreams don't help,
Ella said. We have real problems.
Pieces of ceiling fell revealing
a cupola. I scraped at a bubble
in the wall and found signs of a fresco—
a golden calf. She pulled up a tile
and found another Tomb of
the Diver. Moved the refrigerator—
there were papyri stuffed in the crevices.
Someone's trying to tell us something,
the sink's backed up.

But one can't live like that. I said,
Another world is eating ours down to us.

The space around our own bodies
was difficult *before*. Now the walls
that hid pink dreams grew honest—meaning
solid stone but, at the speed they
receded, thin as air to us,

architraves complicated the hallways
with shadows, foglie were rooting
the doors shut and *Universal Justice* by
different hands was sealing over

every crack. Nothing was redeemed
then with *Sorry* or *I loved*. We just have to
move, she said. And I saw the window
of time left, no bigger than the one
her arms made, tighten.

‡

First Love

We'd been called down, the two of us
and Rumo the cop
to find a missing person or quell a
growing rumor
in the hotel basement, all ductwork and closets.
We split up.
As I approached one dark grate
a set of glowing
eyes approached mine, seething teeth
that lengthened
in my flashlight. Its breath deepened
the source of
our call for certain, filling the chamber
from which it must
I thought, at any instant, burst to
eviscerate us
all. Fixed in its gaze, I could only call to it
meekly: "I desire
nothing, I want—nothing." Again
and chanting:
"I desire nothing, I want—nothing." I could
hear the beast's
anger abate, a cooling suction to. I desired
nothing. But then Rumo
came to my rescue hastily, drawing his firearm—
and the wolf's breath
scorched us. Our certain death
if not for you
dear, lowering the arm, thoughtlessly
tut-tutting:
it's our own, ours, he is ours.

Natio Luporem

Rale the Black Robe to his nephew

Those woods take the place
of a man's mind, wholly: vault it
open, rib it to a point, then
curtain close mazing him
from quiet paths to trip on
roots, more & more trailless for
all its trees.
Like Augustine on his horse, I fought
my desires sidelong to follow the fox after a snowshoe
hare. So slanting, was I often caught on
spokes of pine and thorny cords that drew
blood without breaking
us entirely.
We were cushioned
always by long needles bowering
us, bowing us down. Let's save our breaths
I said, but we lost them quite (like medals in the leaves)
like a thread in thicket.
There it is
the heart seems to warm only
a ground overhead and you hang
among coniferous darks
beneath it. Is it sleep and
force of dream that carries you
further
in and south, falling to rise—?
Only a slap of water or false
step through gelid stream wakes you, all
blistered with fever and neck
raw bitten. Upon this
birth,
nephew, something sure-
footed jars you and, face to face, you
meet your savage. One of you will
have to conquer you now. Which
will it be? is where I blessed
his spear and opened
my coat.

Some Friends From Machigonneⁱⁱⁱ

For every hayloft there is
a couch cushion to break our fall
when we're kids. Now
we get arrested,
we didn't mean to but
shoved her crotch—
we owe child-support.

Our own mothers long since
dead at the hands of
their boyfriends who
woke up in blood
when we learned for sure
the human head could
pulp like anything,

for a while we want to
helmet every little
thing of beauty
like Here, put this on:
see, nothing can hurt you—
feel that, or that?
the entire sky
bent and crackling
around your head
to get in?

It may be a while before
we can coax this one
like a sickly and precious
cousin back out to play—

You're good you're good
we tell him, feel this?
and, No one's going to
take your siskins, though
they explode into the birch
then under the car.

We make him follow us
deep into woods and
up rotted notches
of a pine high over
the Saco, where we tell him

about the last drunk
who died there and
it's okay to be scared

then lead him on into
worse places—our basement
and no adults where
we want to show him
something so badly—
our own bloody teeth
if he'll only make a fist
like this like this, having to
shape the knuckles
ourselves, and begin
to show him exactly what
he can do to us.

China In A Bullshop

No saucer can show its face without
their falling for it
bull of unanswered psalms and
now this bull-
eye to bull's-eye the dreary bull of
Byzantine lolling
too heavy your head bull
of shirked homage
bulls with an unrescuable sister
Ford-competent[iv]
bulls from one beating that race
into the train maw
of the next—like Berrymans who take
their own mugs
wrongly bulls who'd skewer the hand
that fed them
something far too light & gently
in this hour in
too small an arena of kitchen
news' dark tallies
an offer that stings in your nose
of saltpeter
or dirty joke in the sepulcher
and seems to
ask for it like the loving reminder to
"Eat" that asks
for a left horn or the last hope held
out for forgiveness
that always begs for the right.

This is the Breed

anthem

Take Gamba the baker
who carved out a new home at twelve
and the knife itself
take the Champion of the World welding
crooked doors and
the confounded world itself take
your friend Rose who did time for
her would-be bomb-maker
and the bomb itself
our Baptist in his boa and chaps
all those he's saved
and his baptism itself
while we're at it Archimedes
the machinist his civil religion
civility itself
take our Black Shirt
all his sons and daughters
and one daughter alone
Frank's stomach for blood
and our blood itself
Tina's skill with the bones and
our very bones
our songs for the road and
Middle Road in full leaf
Ella's unwavery tastes
and Ella—take
my aim from the garden
and the garden we grew
from *this hill*
in a fit of wild crocuses
honeysuckle walnut trees
whose fallen nuts our dogs cracked
in their teeth
will crack
we would take more than pot shots
more than just hostages'
ears stringing any occupiers' heads
nobles' heads
heads of heads of state

over our bazaar feast day
own funeral
to greet Napoleon's brother
ripe cavalry
with waving arms of flame
and flame itself.

Little Sebago

A lifetime before Newbury wakes up
to find Rita,
calls his buddy for a gun, for himself, having
pummeled her face
to pulp, with his fists he thinks,
this dead woman
invited me out with Steve onto their friends' boat.
She smelled of vodka
or it was the engine. That time or another
we went the long way
around Horse Island.

At the friends' camp, Steve got straight to work,
swinging from rope,
planning to shoot matches off the dock at
some ducklings.
I made a pistol out of a notch of pine
and studied a comb.

At lunchtime, Rita offered lamb's tongue,
which she ate
just like pickles from the jar. I thought,
white as fat roots
in the jar. We heard the gravel when
someone took off
in the van. It's going to be a pretty afternoon,
Rita said and then
Steven, no more matches. I remember her teeth
were perfect squares
then, when she smiled at me.

McCabe's been to the far blood-reaches
and back. Seen a lung
removed with no anesthesia. With no
emotional content
pain's quite tolerable, says McCabe.
We check the x-rays
like this one from Malaysia: a whole fish caught
in a boy's esophagus and
from Nebraska: the view into a woman's head
through the gap of her missing nose.

What do you do after surviving a thousand mixers
of the rhinologists & otologists
the laryngologists, and unforgivable advances
just one on your porch
and earliest tremors in your own hand?

Since giving up the scalpel McCabe adopts assistants
like cadets, he and I
walking the halls like warden & chief hungry
for disobedience—
just one cross look challenging each exam room
to shock us and
try our skills at anecdotal dismissal.

Back a few chapters to Day 1:
Don has to watch it there, he says
as we follow a live feed
from the O.R. He's right by the brain stem.
A red trough.
I don't yet know him but confide in McCabe
about the long hall, the cries
and the boy with the tusk I saw, just now. Ah, yes.
Waves it away.
Our nearness to other species, you know
always waiting to be expressed.

One night in a converted hospital,
I had to share a bed
with the friend of friends and dozed off only to
wake as one
who's begun to slide and jerks up to stop.
I got out of bed
opened the terrace doors—to a woman on the street shouting
"I want my money
you pigs! I want my fucking money!" It went on
for a minute. Two young men had
gotten out of their car with her for some reason. "I want my
money!"
The block welling up but no one changed his mind.
Her shrug's feathers shuddered when
she shot a finger at them. Soon other doors opened around us,
to the left, high above
and below. She wouldn't shut up. There was no
sleeping through this.
All of us, half-naked audience leaning on its elbows, over the
ironwork.
"Are you okay?" someone asked, as though she were
one of us. "My fucking money!"
she went on, the street dumbly flashing its few windows. We
started calling
to the young men. Separate voices, then nearly in concert:
"Give her
the money. Give her her money!"
But the little unaborted high-collared pukes. One
stroked on his phone. The other
gave the woman—maybe nineteen or twenty
—a good shove and
she fell over the curb onto her butt. "You fucks!"
But none of the three looked up.
"You okay lady?" But she didn't look.
The three dumb beasts, they took it
as they must. The momma's boys peeling
away in their car. The girl
lifting her body.

Al Matt'ᵛ

Cracked tooth in God's mouth
             to tear my life
from the pit
             everyone just
teeth lined up
             more or less I paint
my tiger by the mouth
             fangs first
around the tongue
             and throat watch him
bite through
             the picture I am
frightened
             when I paint the eyes
I make a spray
             of whiskers then
stripe the face
             only with grappa
and smoke do I
             settle me down
get a grip
             tell myself
and raise
             an umbrella pine
from the blue
             background yes
call me *Naïve*
             all of my tigers
devour me so
             in a sitting
only then maimed
             my raked soul falls
bleeding out
             trees and reeds enough
to let the Po run
             among them
drag me
             secret in secret
to my brothers
             you.

‡

American Mastodon
learns to speak

any number chase me
deep into
woods again but what face in this
pine's frieze keeps
showing itself—all jointed jagged
near-demeanors
cheekboned brow-shapen
lipped looks
all parted and re-set in the brecciate work
of bark bit by bit
about to speak and now tugs me by
the eye in a
tendon-jerk upward tumbling of
trunk leading
piece to—piece finally catching in
limbwork where
wanting to climb makes an arm
wanting to
grasp makes me fingers wanting
a cone a
thumb and clutch to cradle it having
got so far
in a chamber of breath I hear
my first word
the biting ah or pursed lips
of mmm
ah mm I am for all the hours'
searching
kin to pine who take me
in keep me quiet
like a child hidden in the hem
of a nightgown
when a flung door flies into wall
now *hush*

makes a smoothie

Pa's stuck in Dodge
too busy
for his wife's overneeds sodium tablets water water
watching
Gunsmoke again for signs that
Matt Dillon is
mortal or I'm the one who
asks O 75-inch
won't you show us finally what can crack
the Marshall's law

no one can
control this climate all of us sweating
when the woman appears
screams What am I some animal you leave to die I want to
blow up this house!

I limp like Chester and the frig
opens its arms
to my open arms Gimme something
gimmee
some thing to puree I charge when
it displayeth
nothing only bitter olives filet of haddock
a fit
of ancient grapes shrunken and
climbing back
up into brittle vine

It's going to ruin my one good leg
I think
all this back and forth
but I'm not
Chester haven't been
dragged
near to death by horses no one is
listening
to the other until Dillon
at the deathbed
takes the real Chester's hand
in his own hands and
vows justice Justice for the ones
who done it.

birth story redux

Each day's chance's a foot's
width
and slipping so how can anyone
raise an alarm
or lean-to much less a family or dome
if steadying
the elephantine self's the grandest
feat of balance
death-defying yeah all my feet and
berth of my head's
swinging up on that narrowing ledge
in Gaetano's cave
where the sea swelled in at our feet
its warmth
calling us down from the gelid perch and
cord of light fresh
water ringing from rock
mineral light
I should chapel the air around sing
into the concavity of
and scrawl full of gods gods gods
in my likeness
and yours and his and his.

trompe l'oeil

I caught one of Ligabue's tigers
haunting the den
chewing on a soft volume of Rilke
when he got an idea
in his head sniffed out a Billie Holiday
and threw it
from his maw like a Frisbee then a
Hank Williams but
seemed amenable I mean able to
be reasoned with
if only it could find a color a texture to
appease its gorgeous hunger
those eyes making me precious as Saturn
jittering in its rings
its real curiosity to savor the things of
a Mastodon
it clicked through a souvenir
camera
it scored an unhung mirror with one nail and
naturally
licked its own image no arguing with
that
I'd have given a hind leg to sustain
it but my dear ones
wanted a look and it was no good to
let them ride it
I decided I'd better rid us of the sweet beast
before anyone
got too familiar I imagined the stripes
so soft under my belly
it would have to be done quick just
sprawl down
settle my weight squarely upon it
whatever happened
—Ligabue I never asked to be
the *scuro* to
smother so bright a face.

This guy with the busted walker
whose 40 y.o.
son sat down on the train tracks
to die
whose government's counted
him out
doesn't know the iron & nickel
churning in
earth's core that keeps throwing veil on
veil overhead over
our naked heads impenetrable mostly
to solar winds

"That which you have within you will save you,
that which you do not have within you will kill you"—
O apocrypha!
but try telling that to Bill or Bill's bones

what good's the
magnetosphere to his bewildered
cells
though shielded from all
that radiation
still chased by worry over the pills over his
stolen pin #
over his boy's blood in him is it chasing him
trackward
I'll be damned if I'll go down
easy
armed with his money pouch and that bent
walker he says
I ain't going anywhere.

I read "If this Flag offends you
then you
need a history lesson" and admit
I want history
to lessen to lower my chin permanent
where this one
strap of muscle's been waiting eons
in my jaw
to grow taut again tie my brain up
tight in
a sheep's skull nearly
thinkless

I think this head's poor shelter
as Mr. Wise taught
his 7th grade every fall on the workings
of the speculum oris
through which as slaves we'd have been
force-fed

Did we clench our jaw tooth-
tight against it then
the thumb screws' thread-wise
widening or
only now do I imagine the tongue
pressed
back gagged by a funnel making
my body trough

nothing inalienable to the
bumper sticker
any more than to those ships' surgeons
who found no obstacle
in a shut mouth and no bit of human
cordage that
couldn't be loosened with a little
nerve.

A Dire Wolf's been burrowing down
in me
dare I worship morning's tendril
on your eyelids
dare kiss it lose a breath when
a lowlow moon
unbursting riseth he bristles up
my eye growling
Gone soft gone soft gone soft if
a Bach partita should
follow me to bed he bites real slow
down into
my ripe eardrum riddles it
with pulse
tolerates nothing
but pulse

I reared some ox hearts from seeds that
swiftly tendrilled
toward the window and he jealous
of the light
nosing out my long nose goaded me
Root 'em
up nothing goes unwrenched these days
the gunwise
sense in my extremities that says
You're no man
you're no Man unless—

Dire Wolf doesn't care that I have
no other life
but this like Hawking thinks us
an excrement
of some sky but dreams us up no other
suns beneficent no
pinewoods nor easier prey
only pack-wise
hems all beauty round in the tightening
circles of my ribs

and I let him I let him
cause he hasn't yet seen one quiet boy's
inventions
like this—flame-proof thorn-flower
painted in water-colors
for all I know if it's blooming in me
it will burst
open in Dire Wolf long spears outward
and then who's a man
now that little howler who's the
big man?

☦

Seven Addresses [To The Lord]

I

Praise be to you who will green the hillside
          around the jar of my stunned ashes;
in the meantime
                    of a singed millennium:
thank you, for the blue bath of
          sleep that oranges with day
my body brimming
                    sense and every order
of thought worst & brightest
          as this dark morning in bed
when I'd found the evergreen I'd been hunting for
                    and found I had no axe or saw
to fell it but only the spare house key
          —in *folk tale* maybe potent
as the comb
                    which dropped behind us
would forest up deeply
          to confound our pursuant
and evil godfather, but here
                    praiseworthy for its little teeth
biting into the bark
          surely a life's work, O Lord.

2

I praise your good sense
              to confound me with likenesses
that the first features to break a surface
                    are my mother's
nose and lips followed
              by Sinanthropos' long snout it seems
wide ridge of the brow and lastly
                    FP's notched jaw
though bearded over
              as Thoreau said after passing
hills of razed pine along the Penobscot
                    to feel the world less
exposed I am bearding over nearly
              lost in a nest of messages
if not for her call
                    to the barber
her rsvp to the terrible party.

3

May I gain some wisdom
                    from the thought of niches in tuff
from which pigeons in Orvieto fell
                            through doors in their own
image, air rising up
                    to unshuddering half-spans
of wing perfectly
                        filling the primaries
and secondaries that cupped either side of
                the body's knot
to figure a slow fall into
                            a persimmon tree or
grassy roof of the necropolis.
                    It is the genius
available to each, when his perch
                        grows into fear or want
to re-enter the world made for him
                    or, for the Orvietani in times of siege
cut off from streams and pasture,
                        his willful return
to their columbarium
                to be their food.

4

I confess my faith in
            the outcomes of little tests
to which I pin
                        hopes sincere & foolish

            I must reach the faucet
before the pitcher brims
                        open the creaking door
noiselessly; I must catch
            a feather in my hand
hold my breath to
                        the end of the train;

            I admit to counting on such
means, once wagering
                        on magpies
alighting in odd numbers
            for a child of our own
considered us
                        cursed by evens
when the blood followed.

You who have known
            my growls and fawning
to the washing machine
                        in the car or backyard
my playing numbers
            multiplied by frequency
observing the math
                        also in poems, take them for
what they are—chasing
            figures, like Caesar's deer—
will you begrudge me
                        the wrong woods
and trespassing? Can you?

5

For the undersigned may you
                anoint the rises anoint
the climb ahead of us
                           with little Campione
looking back
              over her shoulder

                         anoint the moss
once knee-deep
             rising and filling
roots—anoint them
                   for waking me to
lurch after her

to sell nothing
                 as dearly
to fern the light that
             itches down
                   in the up-laddering
of woods anoint
             one rung
I could catch bend break
                 and pass singing

             I sing down a world of verticals
more and more heavily
                 the thickest arms
on a bed of needles
             I've rested

                 where the young birches
brighten for our passing but
             out us
amid pine trunks dark
                 as kiln doors.

6

Always drawn to the world's false niches
           and blind windows
dizzying heights fall on me as when
                    I climbed the Laurentian stairs
a thrill of undertow
          while cresting up toward
a columned re-entrance:
                    may I never tire of being
stretched.

May it please you—
          my latest creation story:
that any heart to speak of seems merely
                    the goke at the center
of strands to a shroud-laid rope
          over-
wrung as you've seen a rag twisted
                    over and over: the form
that climbs into a ball
          then falls open
between too distant hands.

7

You who bend light tirelessly
                through matter and antimatter
which physicists trapped in a collider
                      for 1000 seconds[vi]
in order to better see the beginning,

                    if I am to be filter
if I am to be cord-grasses
              through which it is screened
into purer or other
                  forms may you deign
that I know them at least as
                I know my own son
or, if not, that I may feed them
                a little distance.

Grotto To Sebastian

Resilient one, Namesake of my father's mother,
Patron of archers,
Patron of recovery, against the plague against
suffering—or
the strength to eat it, you needed
two deaths finally
to reach Him whose love took, in
your heart, from
a whisper. Patron of spreading fire to
wet branches, confessor
of martyrs, counselor of soldiers—. Patron
of faith answered
with arrows. Patron of
the Lost Cause.

Sealing pain in with swaddling, so blood
pounds the joints
into motion, then no more. Patron
of lifting her head. Patron
of tranquilizers. Patron of being locked
in her room. Of
blue eyes with no ancestry. Being
so beautiful once. Of
asking for just another hour. And another
hour in her room
but without me.

Our bodies floating in the sewer,
and the one who finds us.
Being nursed back. The Lost Cause.
Forgiving your friend-
executioner. 70 times 7 faith answered
with fists. Taking
a beating once and for all. Dying,
listen to me:
for every arrow I have a prayer.
Whom do I seek?

Vitruvian Moon

The breadth of each thing loved
      unloved from
Euphrates to
                  Mississippi nothing
escaping my dimensions
      jumping-
jack of each
                atom and megalith
both measured
      perfectly in my
armspan cast from
              moon's light why
go further
      except for this obedient
and anxious horse
            whose leapsense makes
Earth fresh
      as new apples again warm
as your hair though
           awful the long ladder
counting down
      will you be
watching guess nudge
           the little pool—right
more right since
      one or more feet
for the story of misfalling is old
           will
catch when everything
      falls back into
true shape and density the
           head of one name
pulped against one
      much harder.

Defense of Singleton[vii]

Your Honor, by reason of fathering
his own mother and miscarrying himself

If it please the court, he is a rabbit-
mind high up in tulip tree
when consciousness is nothing,
said an unbidden angel, but chlorophyll—
only color that color sees

Your Honor, the ram in the bramble

Your Honor, the light buoying my head
presses like too little air the bluing infant
into whose face my father breathed
the color back, Your Honor

if it were you in your own arms
one color would uncolor its son; we are guided
by his climbing deeper after tulips
over deepening trajectories

The rabbit, even for ears and acutest
angle of leap-pent legs can be reduced
to sphere, thanks to Grisha Perelman

"Yes, the Poincare was little different
than mushroom hunting but led deeper
into woods. Forget the prize and gathering
of Minds round as their skull-cases.

It's why I've taken you with me
along this gully and deeper for dead elms
whose unsleeving layered with leafthatch
softens chambered hearts of morel."

In a Dark Chamber Rembrandt's Jerome, whose thought
until this instant climbed the winding stair up
into void, frame—nothing, heavy the hand spent
with Pammachius and terrors of *all sight, all hearing,*
all action, all movement

Your Honor in spite of gunpoint or begging any angel can leave you
to your own devices: eight angles of room
fall in like crows I am nothing but sorting
wing from wing-edge all inaction
a day all hand guiding all knife to a woman's neck (so they say)
in the Hamburg grocery all height all fallen
into legs that build me up again (all eye) all jowl
and rooted teeth all tooth then all neck
and the very blue that oranges
where all body enters it all
woolen chest all navel all cock, Your Honor—
if I am to be this alone

So starry eyed you see space roughly seated
before you, strapped with minutes

all minutes

Long Grasses With Butterflies (After Van Gogh)

The helmet is meant to silence
you   calm you   the patient's head
being a thick cross-herding of
thoughts   this method is
slaughter down
to one   with your own blood
pressed snugly
on four sides and strap
around the mouth
it is field
say it is
a garden
say it
is.

‡

Higgs Field Theories

6

In a sanitarium or some bog
　　　　　　along the Po River, jungles
entered the roving mind of
　　　　　　　　Ligabue, leaving
little room for him or
　　　　　　his creatures to escape
their design—this gazelle
　　　　　　　　for instance, leaping
with all four legs blindly
　　　　　　to the edge of the picture plane
will never clear the palms
　　　　　　　　and tall grasses
bristling as the leopard's
　　　　　　fur bristles—the strokes
all hashing in around
　　　　　　　　the awful innocence of that
fleeing soul
　　　　　　that single line.

7

Seen the little houses?
and nearer, their grazing horses—incandescent
grit against the fallout of
Eyjafjallajökull[viii]
cast low? Surely you see each
body lent to
but not lost in
the graining.

Dear cliffs will be ground
to beach, yes yes yes, and my Cumberland, what else—
as far in as Little Sebago, lost
marshing out to a rising sea
but you don't have to
tell me—

just admit you could tell me
apart from the waters
without draining them
where I first dove through green and black
down to lakebottom
awful reeds dragging on
my heels upon rising
and the air snapped, bittering
in the throat, the skull unseized
its brain, its plates riding
no other blood but mine.

I do know the cup of
my senses will drain into
real waters. Does it
change the fact we were
almost a meal one night
for an owl, in Cosgrove, or that
now little A.R. is making rules
for the baby who keeps
dreaming us up
entirely new lives?

8

Is it squandering my bargain
always to carry
around nine copper chalices
standing
in their little copper
saucer—a set
to still me in a shaking house?

to spend a thousand seconds—
more—a whole hour's
worth of ingenuity crouching low
as humanly
possible to lure the half-dead
stray cat (limping
on a busted hip) with string &
soft whispers to
a dish of cream or pinch of fish
between my fingers?

to keep making a clearing for you here
not like a trap where
a shortcut's the thing that costs you
cover so
the weakest sickly smallest doubting of you
are culled away—not
that so much as arrested
by the open
grass-like for panic and asway

we give up
our mother's béchamel or kushari
give up bread as food and
tool give up eating from any certain
earth and gather
at a table set with nothing
but the toy
copper saucer and nine toy
copper cups.

9

In a court document I went
looking for
I find a girl in her hospital room
a girl as you once were.

Recovering from a tonsillectomy
she cannot speak
above a whisper, when the priest I loved as
a father enters
offers to pray with her. Prays

with her
and then tells her what he'll do
and tells her to
bite his knuckles when he goes
under the sheet,
to go on biting his knuckles.

I should curse, wish the worst on him
my Joseph E
who gave me half-dollars & unconsecrated
bread in the sacristy
when I was very young, taught me,
with joy, to follow
the Virgin Mary's example,

who raised goldfinches in the rectory,
Brazilian cardinals,
canaries and Java finches, with great care, speaking
to each
as Francis of Assisi, I imagine, would have
spoken to each.

If the girl survives I ask her
forgiveness.
I have walked into that room,
powerless to
hear his dear voice again and think
of the birds, birds
that must have been paralyzed with
love—and hushed.

10

The swallows, turvy, so often close, never—
We watch from a berm
laid low between their dilapidated tree
and water: their shuttling
between branches, or under our arms, to
skim pools so slightly
to change our understanding of air over water
over us. Always
closest dipping. One swoops now closer. At once
swipes he softly
your cheek. In another way mine. Again, now
deeper. The closer the—
He's trying to tell us something, you say.
They live there
you point, in that dead tree, a radius and ulna
reaching up
out of the marsh with only two bent fingers.
Exit these, precisely
and make what they of us? Still we stay.
And the same swallow
keeps coming, keeps cutting he, deeper
our cheeks.
And neither of us can keep from smiling, neither
so much
as a wing's width moving. Even to bone.
Even to tears,
we wait. We'll take it all—.

II

Now that the Boson's
shown itself,
whatever marbles I have
let them
be smashed into mattering;
let my creek
and little cup appear no more like genies
out of a fog but
spark up as a glass I shattered,
its shard-measure of unnumbered spreading floortiles,
shouting, Back,
to my dear one's bare feet,
Just - get - back!

12

In the heart of my woods
I will open
for you alone a bright circle of
grasses whose
entrance will be guarded by a
seeping maple
and marked by the unearthed cheekbone of
a boulder
with a vein of schorl running north-

south let it be the line
whose crossing comes with a grave new life
a constant clearing like
a beam that follows you through
whatever crowd

in exchange for the sight
of staghorn sumac
a real deer or someone who may
be hiding there
snapping open milkweed
like you watching
listening even to catch the other rocks
coming up for light.

Beautiful Curtains

We move over one another.
   We give off light, greenish.
Phosphorescent. Do I know you?
   I love you here. Oh.
I tilt your head and with you
   watch what rises from us.

Our child is not born
   green. I watch her sleep in our bed
when she is an infant. In the morning
   she is not green, but alarmingly
aged eleven years. She says, Dad, I'm
   fine. Can I go out?

After the screen-door slams I turn
   to look up through sink and sycamore light.
She is in her mid-twenties and holding up her own baby.
   We didn't even name her. I'm sorry. I know.
But the light, for what it's worth, she is
   dancing in pure light.

We are suspended in an observation
   but we are not dead
and our love-making is unlike any love
   of the dead. The feel of you. We aren't dead.
Listen to me. Her name...

When I put my hand on the nape of your neck
   the curtains, suddenly, are glowing. Look, it's real.
They are glowing!
   Stand by them and I'll look at you.
Of course I will tell you.

Moveable Chapel

page 145[ix]

Bassinet

knife   my knife

double-edged knife

I have my knife

It cuts well
　　　　　badly

Crooked knife

That is the custom
　　　　　my custom

I am used to doing this

I have no custom

I have the same custom

I want to go on as I have been

I do not want to repent

To cover

I cover it by hand
　　　　　with an instrument

I cover the child's face

The wind has covered the road with snow

I cover myself

I am not yet...

Let's cover ourselves with my robe.

I am covering a man who is lying down.

I cover him so well no harm can come to him

I walk under the cover of

‡

American Mastodon
to his fading vestiges

O tusks O spits to my opposable trunk how
tossing my head
can swath into crowd forest any traffic or party

or the nagging tune that
only to sway
you name

O tuning fork that in sunlight sends
D-minors
or in rain sends G's down to my toenails

what volumes
of marsh and crosshush of pines did I
displace raked
my earflaps and ribs and washed in
behind me

the dream of
an acre of fruit trees what couldn't I do
if I lived upright
more than reaching the choicest fronds to bellow
a name and lord it
over the other males father an entire nation
you know I would

if my forelegs didn't swing like this
like dead weight
of mute trunks' tolling how mute
how flat the world
without you my trunk you blind eye and lip
you periscope
stretching higher the deeper I felt
you trumpet
and flag-waver drooper grasper sprayer the swifter
I dive who plume
the air the loss of which proves these hands
poor heirloom
poor heirs to you cup and straw together

and more than any O straw tail who
sprouted in clay hills
and kindle even in bog in snow you spark meter
you swaying fuse
smolderer chasing me from boat ride to bone school
you metronome
beating 4-3 on my haunches
as my little ones who squeal after and flicker me
ahead of and back to
my sole self haloed and singed
anew anew.

Pompeiian

the secret is always that you are not
perishable
safe away in your boat crossing the gulf except
the heirloom
toy dog or left on a sill the remedy
for an earache
calls you back in the lull between
fallout
and cloudfall I'd go back
and you can
too let's go and ages later our forms will defy
the glum diggers
expecting arms slung over our faces hands
thrown up
against the sudden house-search turning up
nothing nothing whatever
but the gesture of sipping a teaspoon
of Belladonna
your near-speaking lip cinema or one of us
turning the key
to watch that dog flip and flip God
how loud the
unseizing in its belly how it still
scares us
half to death when all four legs stick
the landing.

beast to beest[x]

Your will's never sapped but you will
crumble in
on your own knees your spine eventually
torque and split
that is something and in the meantime it is
really something to see
that elliptical swing of your forelegs and
soft-planting
of each foot down each foot
down.

Dumb self-herder you crashward
pneumatic
tube-work of a beest you corps of
blind marching
how I envy the elliptical swinging of
your calf-tubes
and all your soft-planted feet

though you will never know
the knot
inside nor drag the bloodless meat
of each foot
laughing through gelid water having followed
the glow of
plankton through thinning waves
hand-in-hand
with someone you love you'll never
know the blood-
rushes and sweet undoing of that
knot
to regain feeling in your toes.

Your maker
thought of you long before you were born and
nearly lost to
the world's blind motions lovingly—desperately

tuned your design
abandoned the tape for a blow-torch and with
jigwork
turned out excellent joints for you
cell by cell—.

He thought of that soap-drip to flush
the grit and salt
from each joint thought of a proboscis like mine
whose suction choked
by water would flip the switch and send you
back back to terra firma.

Could you
care less to be pulled back or would you
just as soon
be dragged out to some shelf then
dropped
weightless to the seafloor and ground
to splinters

as though gravity could grow with
rising water
acidity rising who knew to usher
our decline
along with the colossal sperm whale
whose echolocation
can rupture a human eardrum and
collapse
human lungs you know they call
swimming
with sperm whales suicidal—
such curious giants
who merely to say to one another
Behold—

this small creature!
kills us
with one crack of an inmost chord

pierceable heart
pierceable drums these are the things
you mute
scaffold faithless pilgrim impossibly
remote
to you the pierceable eye that lifts to

take in lesser
lights as a depth and the greater
lights as shallows
to enter with all crests between
and judge

the speed of the world's approach
just how much
it wants to know you—or
doesn't

you gorgeous imbecile
how I envy you
the nearness of your maker—Jansen harried
by wind and who hates the wind
but pays every homage shrining up sails
for you to it

what I'd give (just once)
to drift like you under the sails of myself
sails sensitive
enough to catch any wisp already
now if she whisper
me a number any number I'd shed my
winter weight
all weight if she whisper my name
into my giant ear
and we'd evolve us a daughter her name
a stratum
of rock enough to hold our bones.

about the illusion of one body

To admit the star Mirach knows
nothing of
Alpheratz though we join them
in one body
and call it *Andromeda*
now that I've seen
the drainline milked by pinching it first close
to the wound
my belief in this body is a matter of forgetting
depths—

the shoulder is nothing
else and the hand pushing up from bed
the mouth forgetting
the body's claim to it unless we say—
I know she is more
than an instant of light dragged by cloud
across to
dwell in a field or this
living room

Remember the virga
that carried a body east over Cosgrove by
the joints?
head hanging with dragging legs
then in an instant
only a handsworth of sun dissolving
on a near hill
that shed its grasp when
dragged further
into the open—exactly how she is
daring me
not to believe when she's studied
her own bones in
the mirror and very carefully
even gently
asks Do I scare you?

family reunion

Is it poring over grit to find
a few grains
is it all these children's divorces
we read already
in their too smooth faces all their
emptied houses
earthly chances and arrests to
tally so
many kisses goodbye that warms us
with love for
one another swiping photo after photo
but dwelling
on this one and cousin Paul's
eyes as if
from that still unblighted living-
room they were
blind all of them to the likes
of us.

to a poet dying young

Did you ever listen for drops working
downward
through the leafwork of a tree I have and
practiced catching
drops from the doomed ash tree open-
handed

and with light touches
I have practiced balancing tomato cans
it's a wonder
all teetery their thirst for light
brimming
from one lip into another
brimming
one mouth to another.

Now I've got this secret antidote
a lot like oil
or purepure drops of vitamin
D
caught in maidenhair spleenwort I saw just
before they
broke from the sandstone awnings
fell into
near total dark and were carried
off

or like ancient microbes that consumed
methane from
the sea floor and formed it into
pedestals still
lifting columns of water off the coast of
Zakynthos
columns that uphold permanent
temple shot
through with godly light it's
true

maybe it is true you've got to dive down
for a growing
fraction of your daily life submerged
half-
blind and cold digging through current
to stay down

I've practiced but can't ever
stay down
more than four lengths nearing
the wall cracking
open to see bubbles useless
as blue
seeds caught in blue
glass

I don't know if death will sink
in
or expel us like air into
air
all lost or all found more
wholly

but in you let
it gather like heirloom
beads more
precious the longer they are
held in
your body oh not like the
Greedy Cup
that filled invisibly
drains
when it reaches a certain
depth
and the trick was never
in your hands
one vessel into another
your life
was never in your hands.

ENDNOTES

i   Burned into the side of an unfinished boat found at the abandoned Fort
Crevecoeur, originally built by Sieur de la Salle in 1680, on the east
bluff of the Peoria river valley.

ii   JDAM stands for Joint Direct Attack Munitions; "moral lights" was a
phrase used by Abraham Lincoln in a debate with Stephen Douglas
that took place in Galesburg, Illinois, October 7th 1858.

iii   Machigonne was the Abenaki name for present day Portland, Maine.

iv   The phrase "Ford-competence" derived from a capital murder case
Ford v. Wainwright, 477 US 399 (1986), whereupon Justice Lewis
Powell affirmed a "constitutional minimum" with regard to Florida's
obligation in assessing Alvin Ford's awareness of his impending
punishment.

v   The "crazy one," after Antonio Ligabue, so-called Naïve Italian painter,
1899-1965.

vi   In June of 2011, at the CERN Hadron Collider near Geneva Switzerland,
physicists trapped antimatter for 1000 seconds.

vii   Charles Laverne Singleton, who was medicated with anti-psychotic drugs
by the State of Arkansas and thereby found sane enough to execute
early in 2004, as reported by Scott Loftis on January 7th in the Pine
Bluff Commercial.

viii   Volcano in Iceland, whose eruption in April 2010 disrupted air traffic
across western and northern Europe for six days.

ix   Taken from Sebastien Rale's French-Abenaki dictionary (currently
housed in Harvard Library's special collections), these are his French
entries from page 145, translated into English with the generous help
of Dr. Caesar Akuetey.

x   After the kinetic sculptures called *strandbeests* by Dutch artist Theo Jansen.

Thank You

To Carol Guerrero-Murphy. To Jorie Graham and James Galvin. To Peter Orner, my favorite storyteller. To Monica Berlin, for years. To Jeff Baker, for the bike ride. To Donald Revell, Vievee Francis, D.A. Powell, Christopher Salerno, Caryl Pagel, and Gabriel Levin, for their examples and generosity. To Greg Terrill, for the desk & road atlas. Sean Cocco, Colt Valenti, Fr. Gregory Kandt, Gina Franco, Natania Rosenfeld, Mary Crockett Hill, Mark Holmes, Sherwood Kiraly, Janet Goodhue Smith, Maria Rosaria De Bueriis & Gaetano Schiavo, collaborators and friends afield.

To Jeffrey Levine, Kristina Marie Darling, and Cassandra Cleghorn, as well as Hope Wabuke, Kristen Case, and V. Joshua Adams. To David Rossitter, for his great good humor and ingenuity. To Allison O'Keefe, for her keen eye.

To The University of Iowa Writers' Workshop, for a Michener fellowship given in Paul Engle's name. To the J. William Fulbright program, for that first year in Italy. To Knox College, for many years of support.

To my Regiacortes, without whom there are no poems: Luigi, Patricia, Gina & Frank; Gianluigi, Andre, and especially Sunshine.

ACKNOWLEDGMENTS

My thanks to the editors of the following journals:

"American Mastodon – *wades through security*," appeared in *Bennington Review*

"American Mastodon – *Nous somme tous sauvages*" (by another title), "American Mastodon – *domesticus*" (by another title), "American Mastodon – *ponders the flowers of his youth*, "American Mastodon – *in which the conceit of himself weighs on his prospects for happiness*, "American Mastodon – *to his fading vestiges*," and "China in a Bullshop" appeared in *Descant*

"Higgs Field Theory 1" (by another title), "Seven Addresses [to the Lord]" parts 1, 2, 4 & 7 appeared in *Mary*

"First Love" (by another title), "This is the Breed – *bestiary*" (by a different title) appeared in *New American Writing*

"This is the Breed – *anthem*" (by a different title), "This is the Breed – *live feed*" (by a different title), and "Long Grasses with Butterflies" appeared in *Fifth Wednesday*

"Vitruvian Moon" and "Defense of Singleton" appeared in *Copper Nickel*

"Grotto to Sebastian" appeared in *New Orleans Review*

"Grotto Expanding at an Accelerating Rate" (by a different title) appeared in *14 Hills*

ABOUT THE AUTHOR

Nicholas Regiacorte was born and raised in southern Maine. Since that time, he's lived in Florida, gone to college in Virginia, worked on roofing crews, worked in a deli, and earned his MFA in poetry from the University of Iowa. He's had the good fortune to live in Italy, once on a Fulbright year in Campania, the second time as a Visiting Professor in Florence. His poems have appeared in *14 Hills, Copper Nickel, New American Writing, Descant, Bennington Review,* and elsewhere. He currently teaches at Knox College, in Galesburg, Illinois, where he lives with his family.